AF598845

AND OR THE

Serge Gavronsky

chaxpress2022

ISBN 978-1-946104-35-9

Chax Press
1517 N Wilmot Rd no. 264
Tucson Arizona 85712-4410

Chax Press books are supported in part by individual donors and by sales of books. Please visit *https://chax.org/membership-support/* if you would like to contribute to our mission to make an impact on the literature and culture of our time.

Acknowledgment: All artwork in *And Or The* is by Constance Lane.

AND OR THE

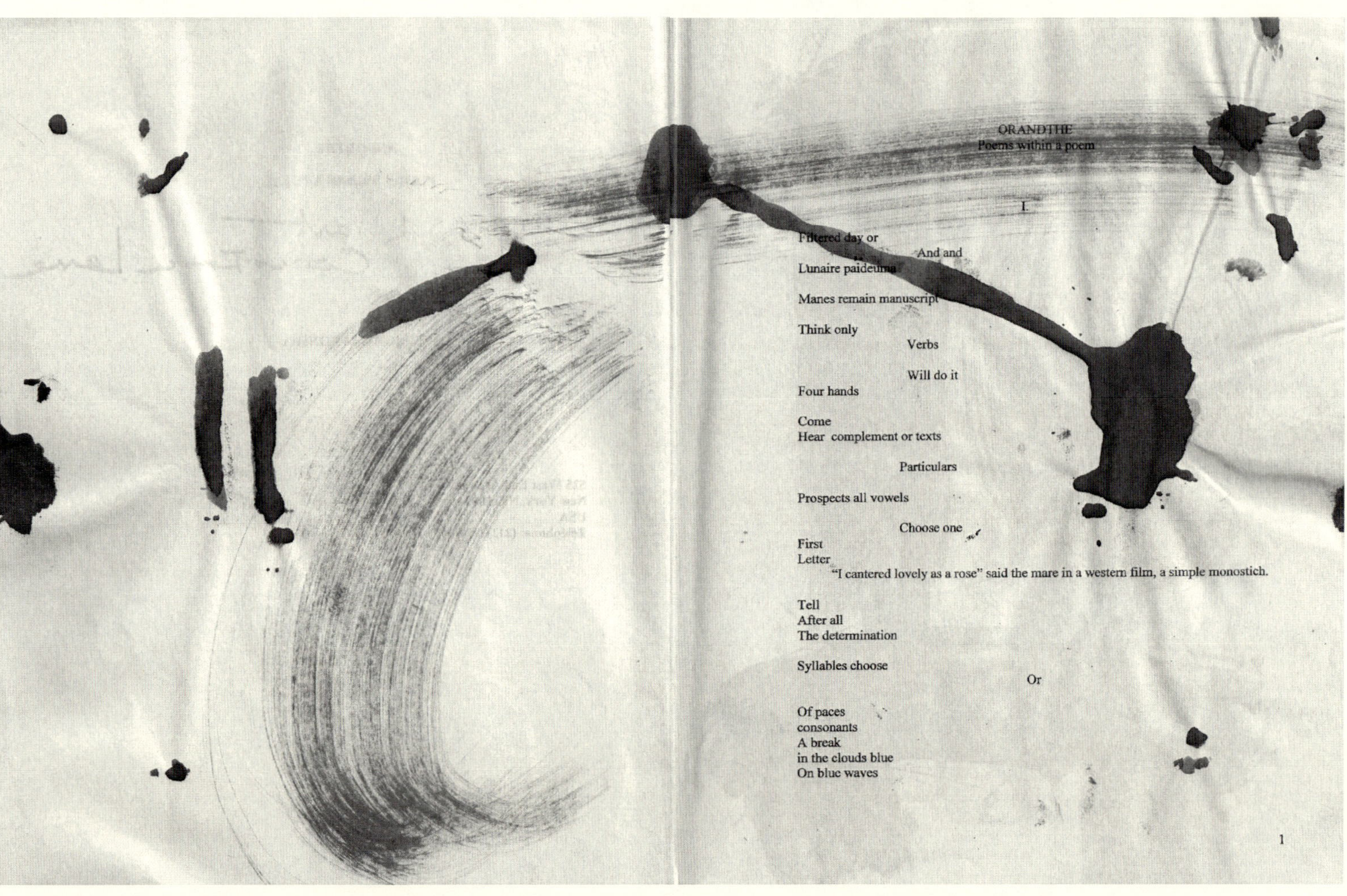

ORANDTHE

Poems within a poem

I.

Filtered day or
                And and
Lunaire paideuma

Manes remain manuscript

Think only
        Verbs

        Will do it
Four hands

Come
Hear complement or texts

        Particulars

Prospects all vowels

        Choose one
First
Letter
    "I cantered lovely as a rose" said the mare in a western film, a simple monostich.

Tell
After all
The determination

Syllables choose
                Or

Of paces
consonants
A break
in the clouds blue
On blue waves

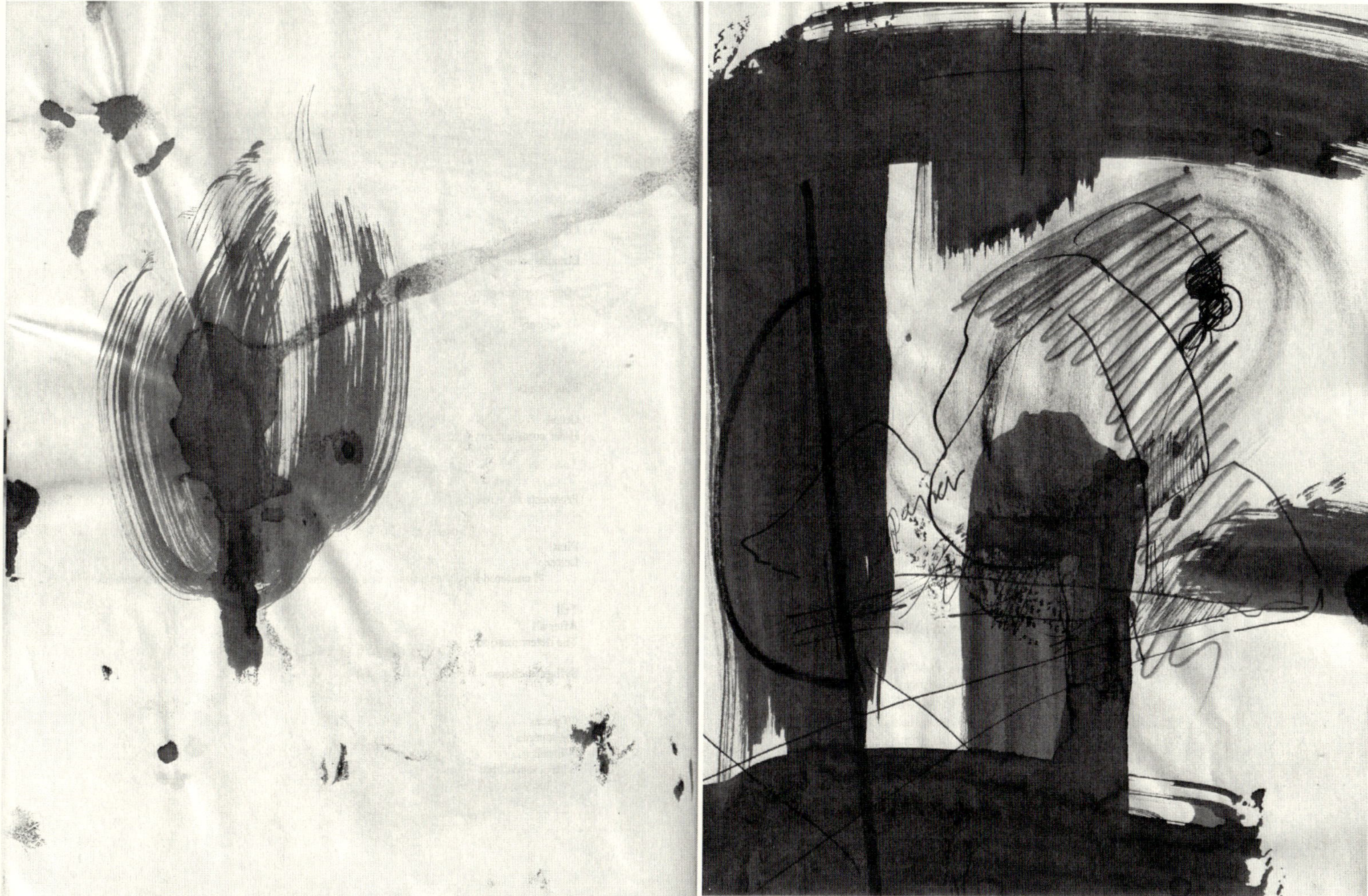

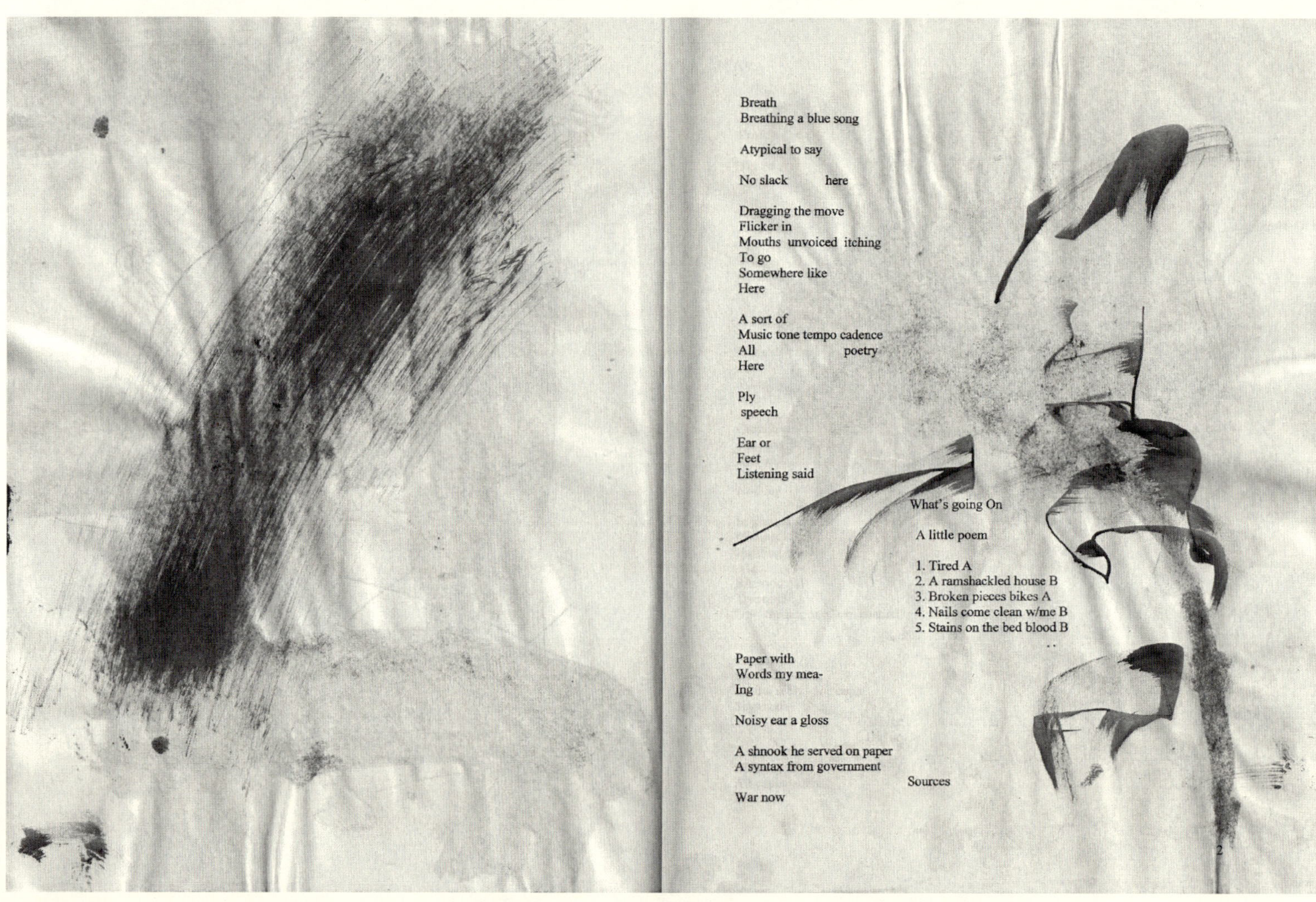

Breath
Breathing a blue song

Atypical to say

No slack   here

Dragging the move
Flicker in
Mouths unvoiced itching
To go
Somewhere like
Here

A sort of
Music tone tempo cadence
All   poetry
Here

Ply
speech

Ear or
Feet
Listening said

What's going On

A little poem

1. Tired A
2. A ramshackled house B
3. Broken pieces bikes A
4. Nails come clean w/me B
5. Stains on the bed blood B

Paper with
Words my mea-
Ing

Noisy ear a gloss

A shnook he served on paper
A syntax from government

Sources

War now

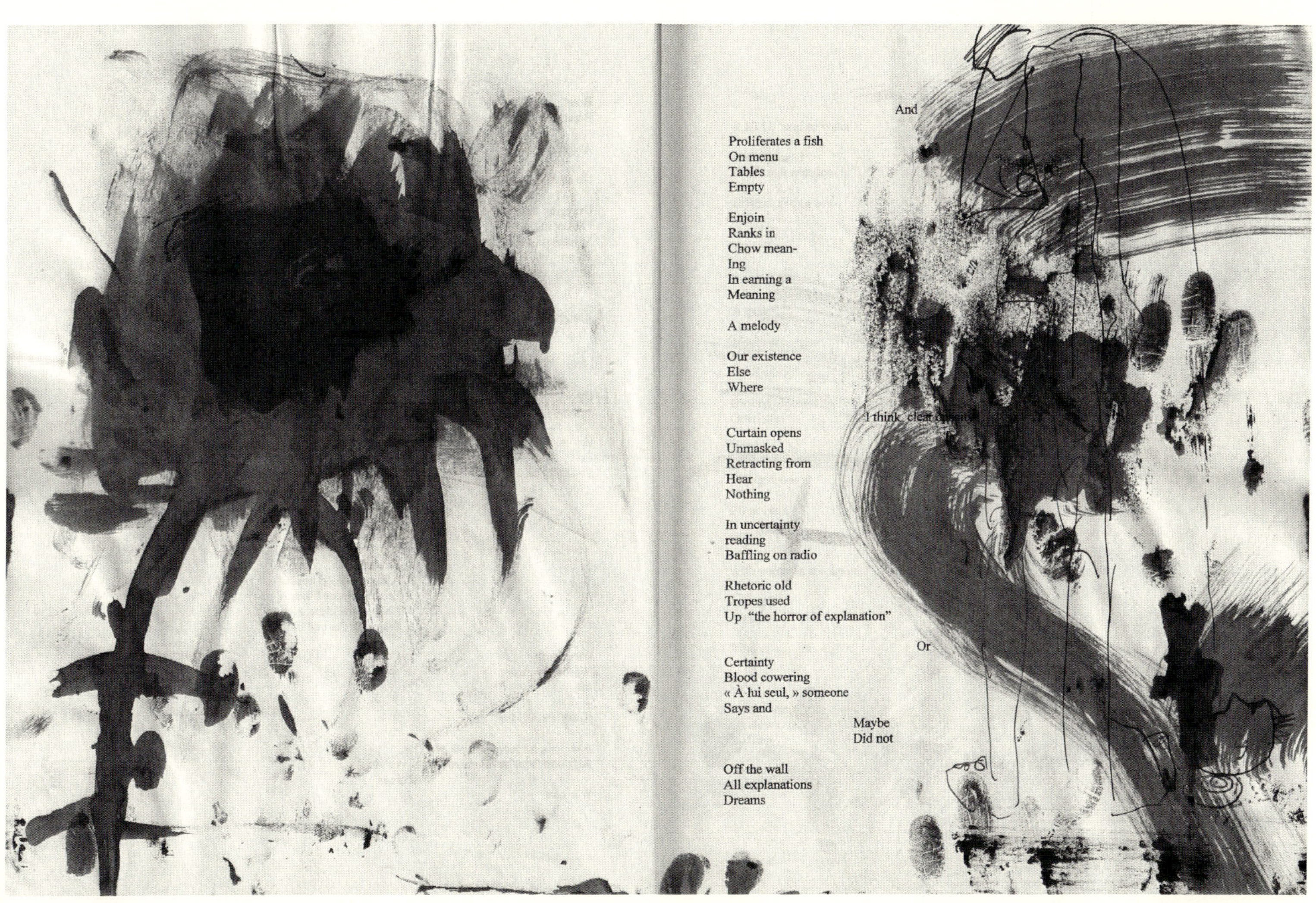

And

Proliferates a fish
On menu
Tables
Empty

Enjoin
Ranks in
Chow mean-
Ing
In earning a
Meaning

A melody

Our existence
Else
Where

I think clear [illegible]

Curtain opens
Unmasked
Retracting from
Hear
Nothing

In uncertainty
reading
Baffling on radio

Rhetoric old
Tropes used
Up "the horror of explanation"

Or

Certainty
Blood cowering
« À lui seul, » someone
Says and

Maybe
Did not

Off the wall
All explanations
Dreams

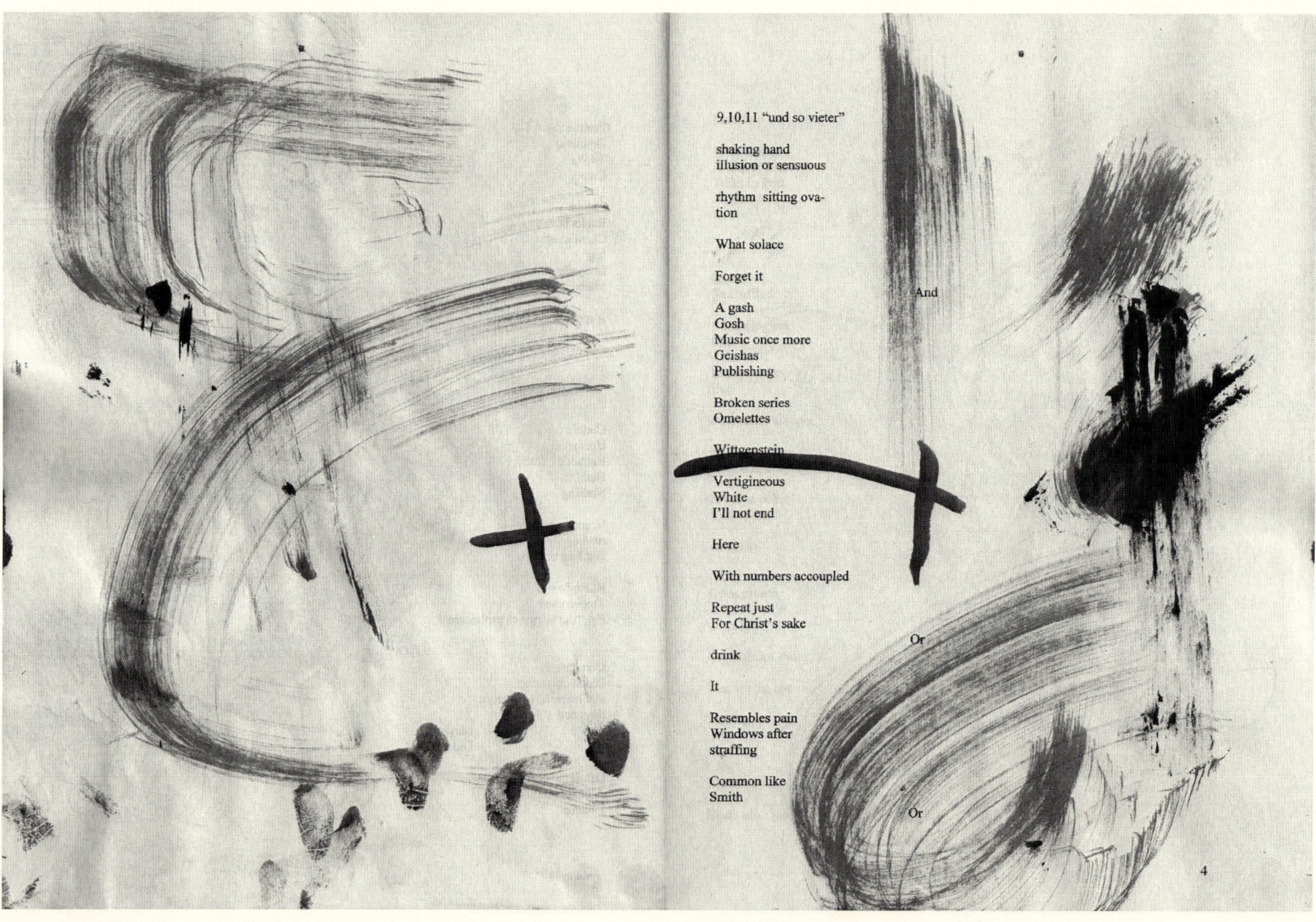

9,10,11 “und so vieter”

shaking hand
illusion or sensuous

rhythm sitting ova-
tion

What solace

Forget it

And

A gash
Gosh
Music once more
Geishas
Publishing

Broken series
Omelettes

Wittgenstein

Vertigineous
White
I’ll not end

Here

With numbers accoupled

Repeat just
For Christ’s sake

Or

drink

It

Resembles pain
Windows after
straffing

Common like
Smith

Or

Lefebvre

Wise manes
A picket fence
Talks in Port
Jefferson

The

Inland
Sea ruffled

Cosmological
bridge

Except for the
Ear

Permanent fixture

Marbles in mouth
To speak lawyerly

Erupt in color
Syncopated

Abyss on

And

Open mouth
A place made
Of paper

Or platform shoes

Resonating eye

This day

For old
Men
Nuttin' doin'

Death ain't proud

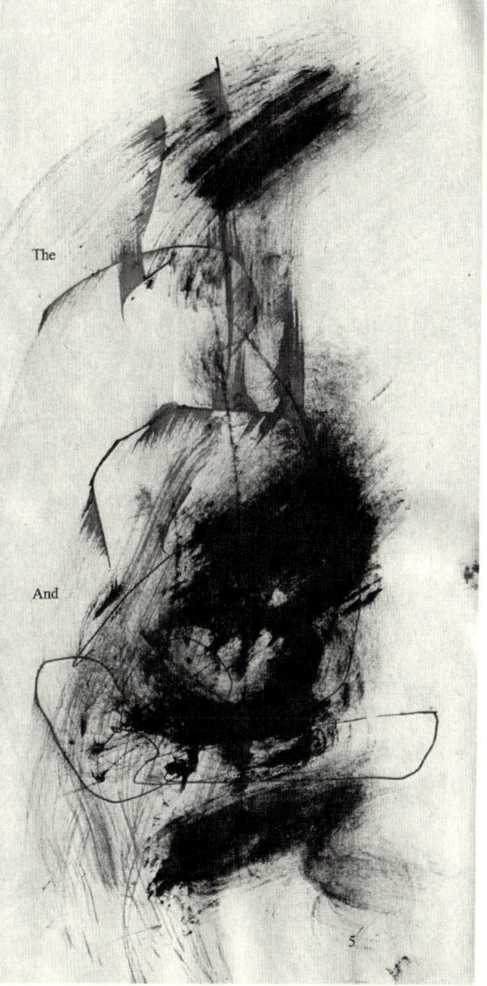

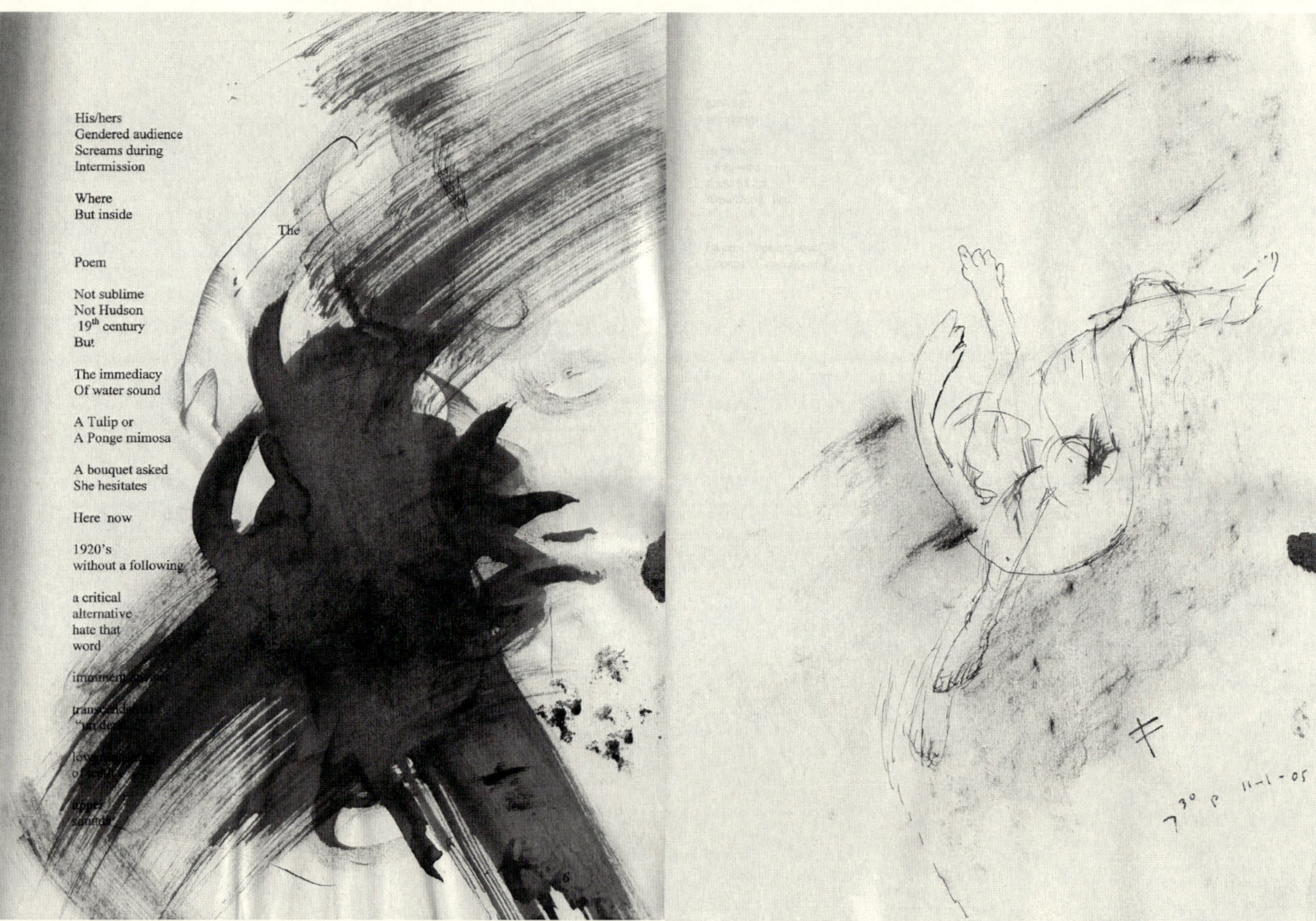

His/hers
Gendered audience
Screams during
Intermission

Where
But inside
The

Poem

Not sublime
Not Hudson
19th century
But

The immediacy
Of water sound

A Tulip or
A Ponge mimosa

A bouquet asked
She hesitates

Here now

1920's
without a following

a critical
alternative
hate that
word

/immanen[illegible]

transcend[illegible]
"un de[illegible]

lo[illegible]
o[illegible]

upper
sounds

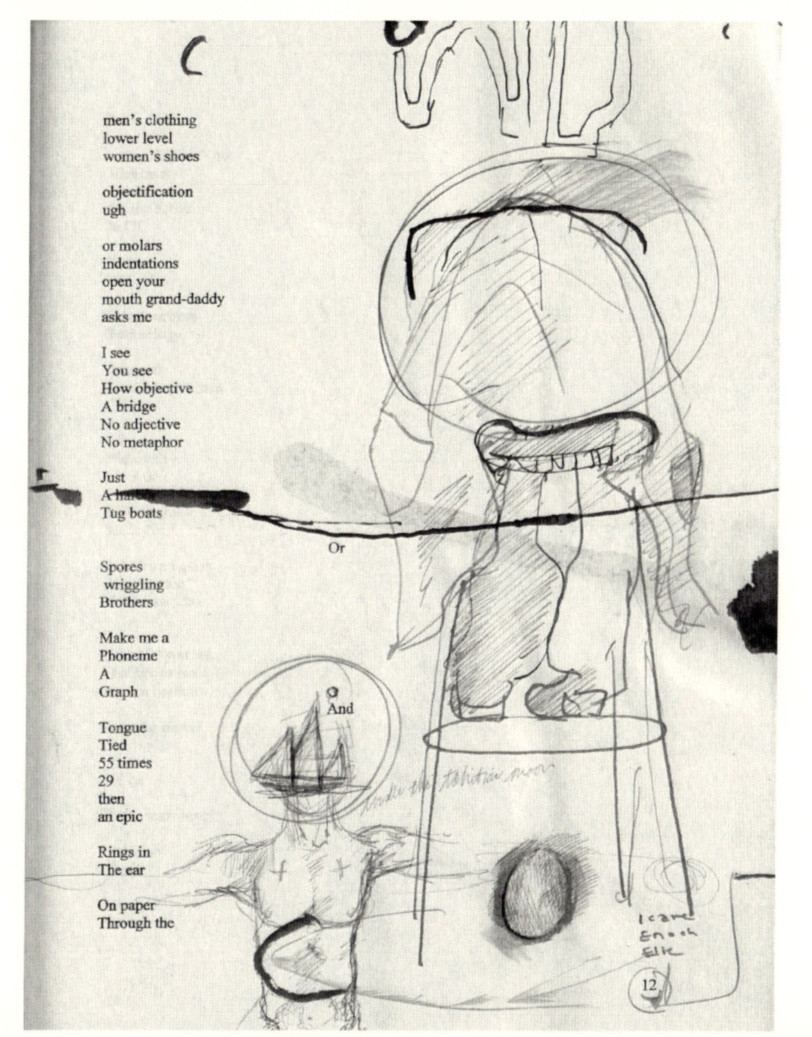

men's clothing
lower level
women's shoes

objectification
ugh

or molars
indentations
open your
mouth grand-daddy
asks me

I see
You see
How objective
A bridge
No adjective
No metaphor

Just
~~A ha~~
Tug boats

Or

Spores
wriggling
Brothers

Make me a
Phoneme
A
Graph

And

Tongue
Tied
55 times
29
then
an epic

Rings in
The ear

On paper
Through the

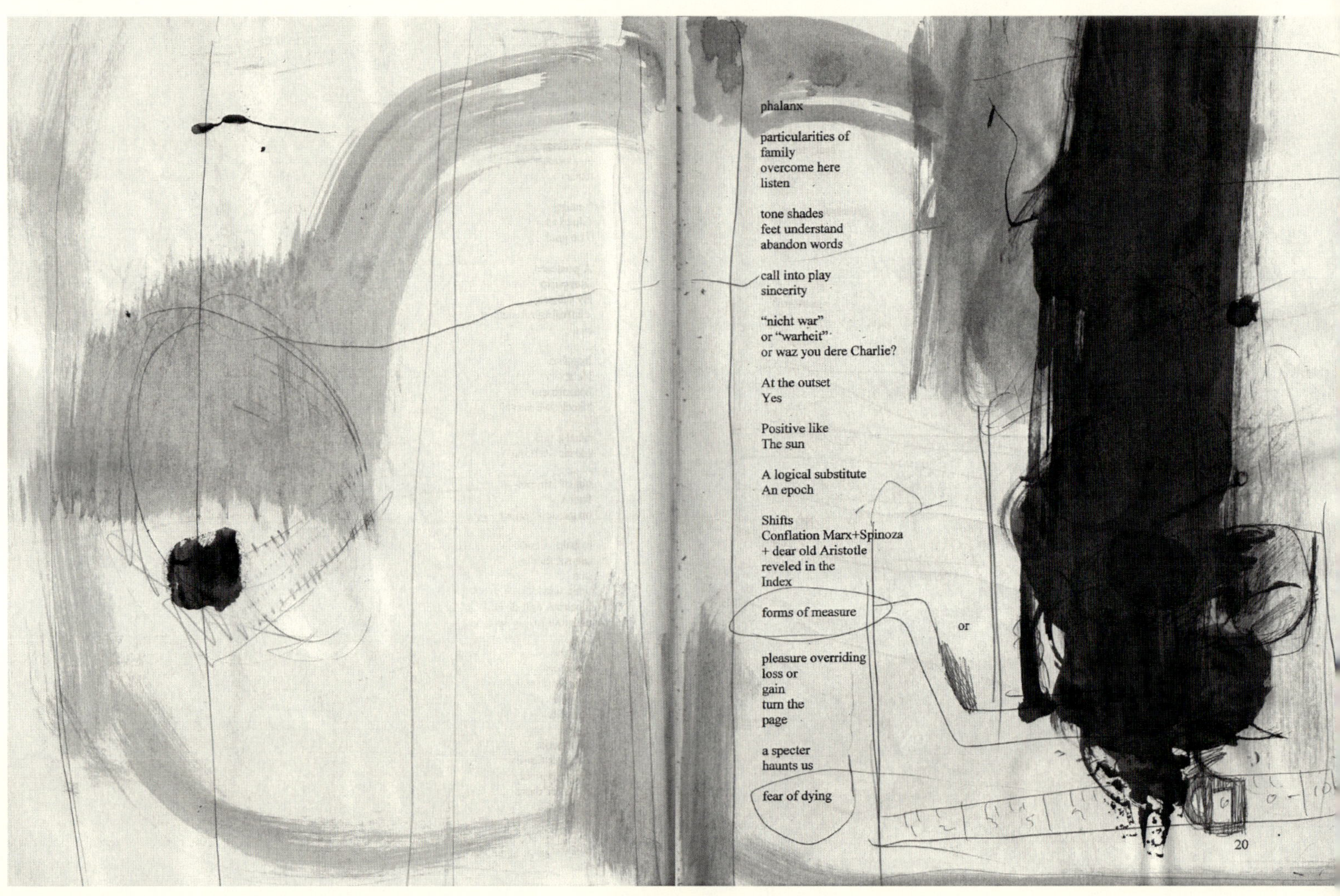

phalanx

particularities of
family
overcome here
listen

tone shades
feet understand
abandon words

call into play
sincerity

"nicht war"
or "warheit"
or waz you dere Charlie?

At the outset
Yes

Positive like
The sun

A logical substitute
An epoch

Shifts
Conflation Marx+Spinoza
+ dear old Aristotle
reveled in the
Index

forms of measure

or

pleasure overriding
loss or
gain
turn the
page

a specter
haunts us

fear of dying

collapsing libraries

all then
meaningless

a day

a day of mourning

only

The

Timorous
Will know.

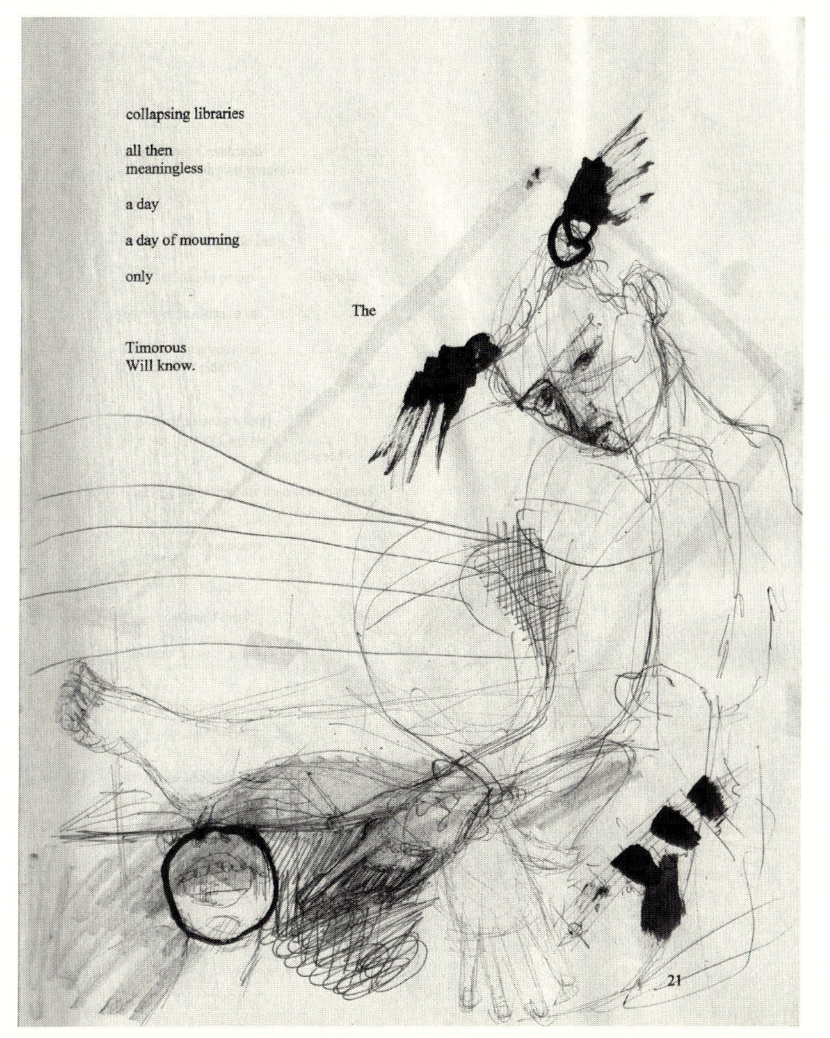

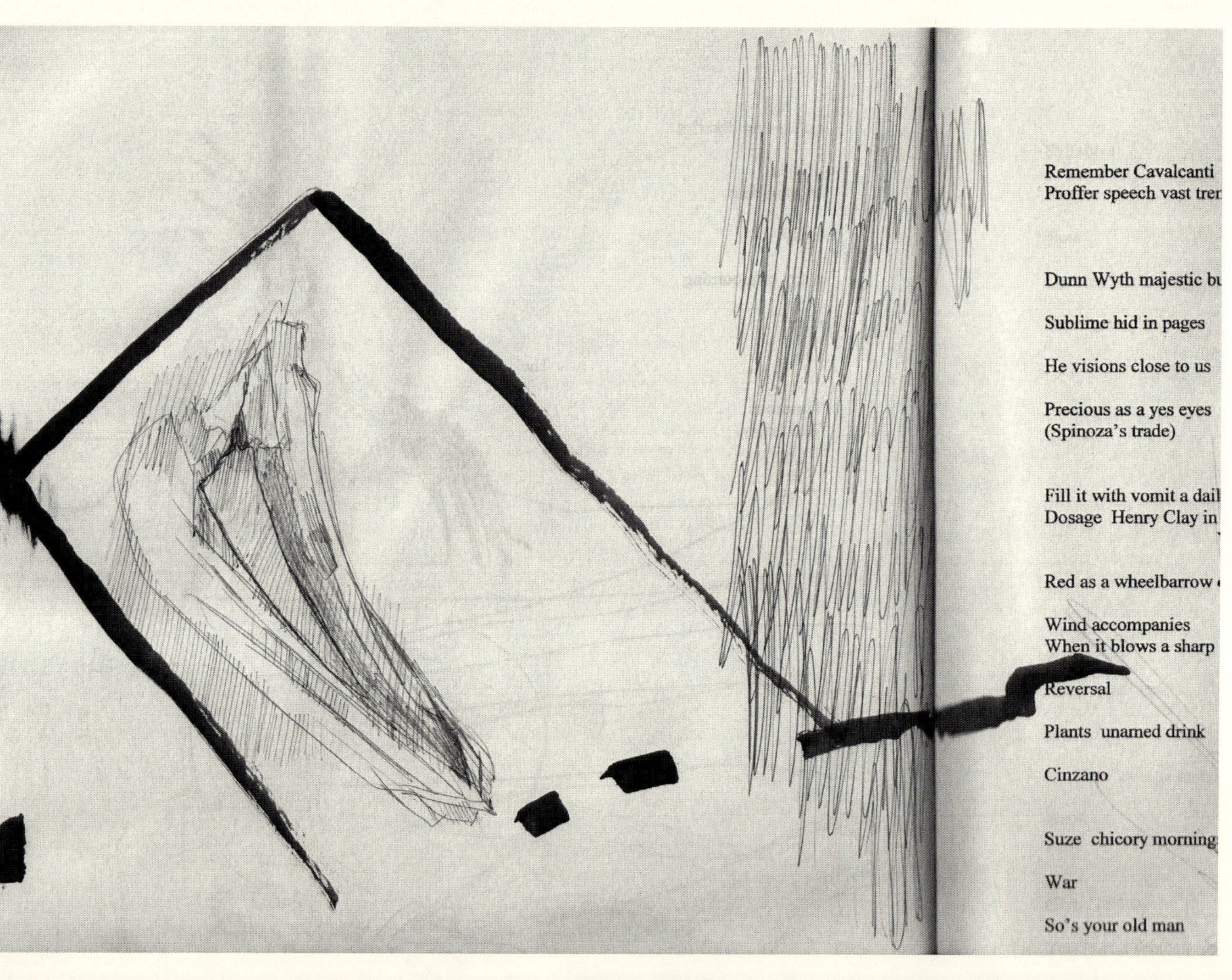
Remember Cavalcanti
Proffer speech vast tre
Dunn Wyth majestic b
Sublime hid in pages
He visions close to us
Precious as a yes eyes
(Spinoza's trade)
Fill it with vomit a dai
Dosage Henry Clay in
Red as a wheelbarrow
Wind accompanies
When it blows a sharp
Reversal
Plants unamed drink
Cinzano
Suze chicory morning
War
So's your old man

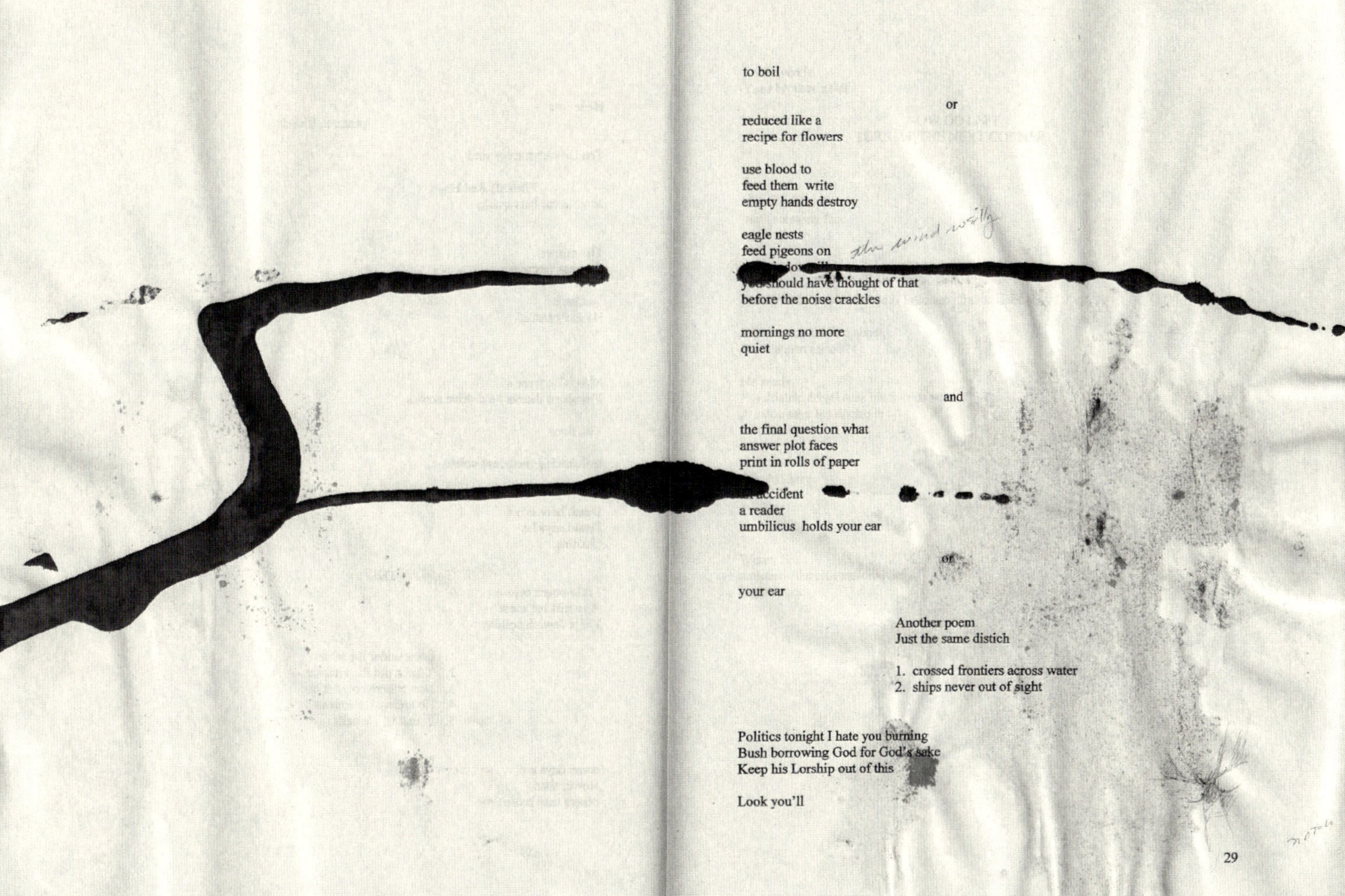

to boil

or

reduced like a
recipe for flowers

use blood to
feed them write
empty hands destroy

eagle nests
feed pigeons on
[illegible]dow[illegible]ill
[illegible] should have thought of that
before the noise crackles

mornings no more
quiet

and

the final question what
answer plot faces
print in rolls of paper

[illegible] accident
a reader
umbilicus holds your ear

or

your ear

Another poem
Just the same distich

1. crossed frontiers across water
2. ships never out of sight

Politics tonight I hate you burning
Bush borrowing God for God's sake
Keep his Lorship out of this

Look you'll

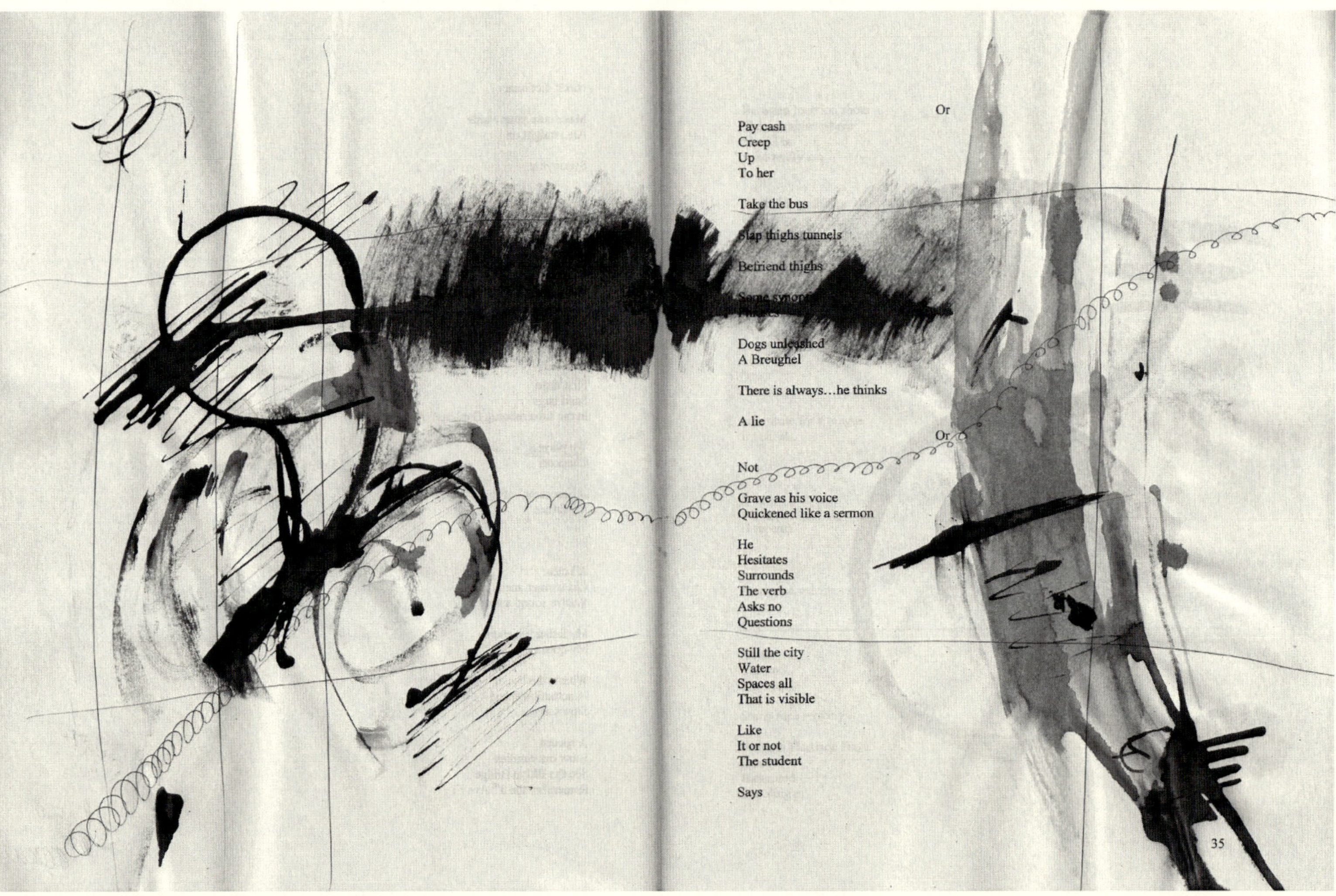

Or

Pay cash
Creep
Up
To her

Take the bus

Slap thighs tunnels

Befriend thighs

Some synon[illegible]
[illegible]

Dogs unleashed
A Breughel

There is always…he thinks

A lie

Or

Not

Grave as his voice
Quickened like a sermon

He
Hesitates
Surrounds
The verb
Asks no
Questions

Still the city
Water
Spaces all
That is visible

Like
It or not
The student

Says

Between location shots
She mumbles where
Shall I be
Who really am
I

Were things things
Finally
Not parts of
Speech

Like blackberries

Or

Pause

"man"

the

substitute for a tongue
in: cheek

heads

or

tails
any questions?
(I repeat)

Yet here a
Line
Drawn across the

Page

Gone
The and
The else

Stony face reciting

William Harrison Hayes
In his
Basement
Drooling at

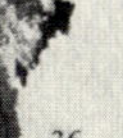

An open mouth breast
In a movie
He condemns
Keeps on
File

Here this

Where once

Or

Before Olmstead's CP

Houses people churches cemeteries

Now doubly dead.

Who will dig up their bones
Make the plea

Filled

Will it be said loudly

And

Irascible (what a word!)
To pow pow
Anger

The

Longish poem right here:

1. But now count syllables
2. An alexandrine four
3. Of them in a rowboat
4. Whence the saying he goe
5. Or again she goeth
6. Toward a pleasant senseless
7. Dicing, knuckle-bones all
8. In a familiar tone
9. What sex she claims outloud
10. He says knows beasts knows beast

Old charm Old country

Similar to his mind
Words like wood burn
Quietly

Or

Love

Leaves sometimes
By the front door

For God alone
Keeps up
With you

And

We have a secret garden
Your body as troubadours
Sang it

XVII.

Dear Professor T.R. Aitre,

Professor Gavronsky highly recommends him (Yale, summa come Loudly) in his letter to our committee's attention (you as a senior professor and a specialist in Lacan's theory of the mirror as well as Professor J.N. Saikoi who has been hard at work on Franco-Vietnamese relations). Together with our two younger colleagues (both of whom have already demonstrated tenure-level production, the first comparing Baudelaire's Poe to Mallarmé 's and the other working on Char's Caws), we should be able to wrap things up at our next meeting which I have called for October 21.

Many thanks for your prompt reply and, just in case you cannot make it, please let me know.

« Bien à vous, »

P.D. Ophile

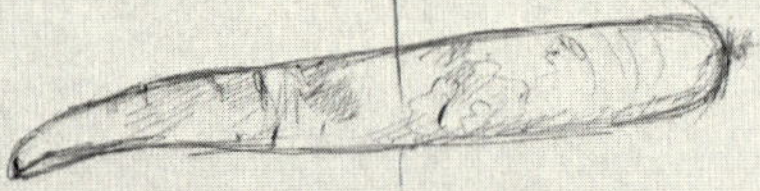

Cher collègue,

I thought I had previously told you that I shall be way that day attending a world conference in Saigon on the Vietnamese novelist Pham Duy Khiem. And to quote the much esteemed Léopold Sédar Senghor, "c'est une communauté spirituelle, une *noosphère* autour de la terre…que j'appelerai la *francité* ». I'm sure within the next decade our author shall be translated in numerous languages (the Japanese have already indicated their interest). He is now compared not only to Proust but to Joyce and Nathalie Sarraute. My own paper addresses the question of cross-current influences between his topics and 13th century Chinese literature in its religious manifestations. I shall return by the end of the fall semester.

Bien à vous,

J . N. Saikoi

Cher T.R.

De mon coté (forgive the missing accent but my Toshiba doesn't have one yet), je dois vous avouer que cette date ne me convient aucunement car je dois me trouver à Paris assister à un colloque international portant sur les interprétations lacaniennes du miroir. Elizabeth Roudinesco compte y etre de meme que Luce Irigaray et Marie Delcourt. Quant à moi, et j'ai heureusement déjà écrit mon papier, je pense qu'il va radicalement repenser le prépuce.

Cordialement,

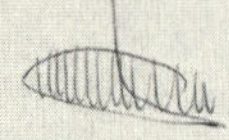

enough of Plato or was it
Aristotle?

Silence in fields of corn
Imitates itself
Where words sing
Sketch out other
Words the spinal split
In Mallarmé's Book

Silence again
He prepares a
Concert his arm hurts
So does his bank account
Today when the
Dow leapt downward
Was that his querry
The original or just
An Imitation

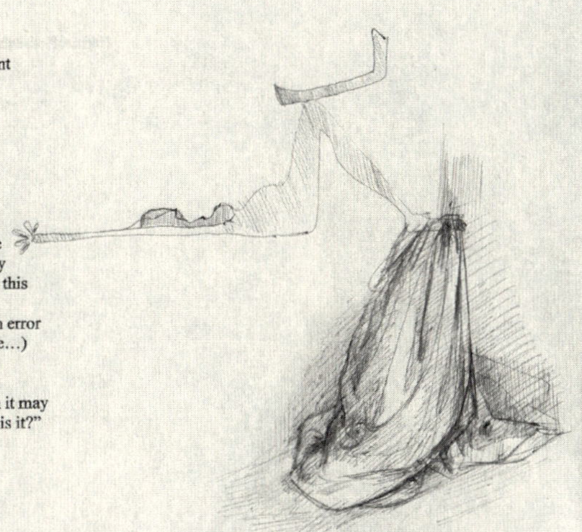

Further down this page
A signature
Someone actually wrote
This unnecessary cruelty
Forcing our attention to this
Inaugural mistake
This *hamartia* (call it an error
Or what you will it to be…)

This I believe is
A good example though it may
Beg the question "what is it?"
"What does it mean?"

Even a poem imperfect
As it is answers you
Your quest is it ever
For truth

Or

The making of truth
Unresolved perhaps
Flawed a circular fountain
In some hotel's front lawn
Or in one of Tati's films

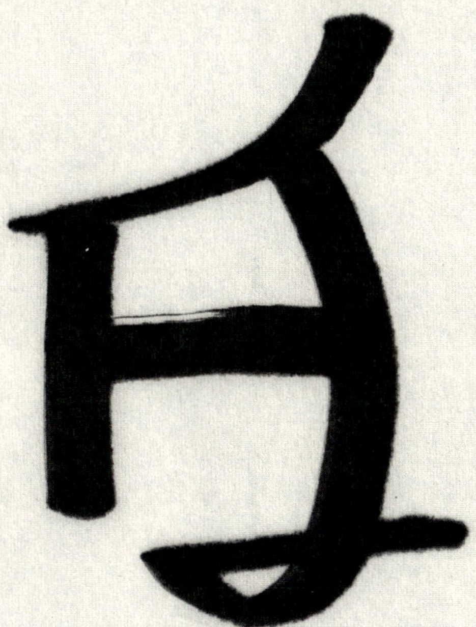

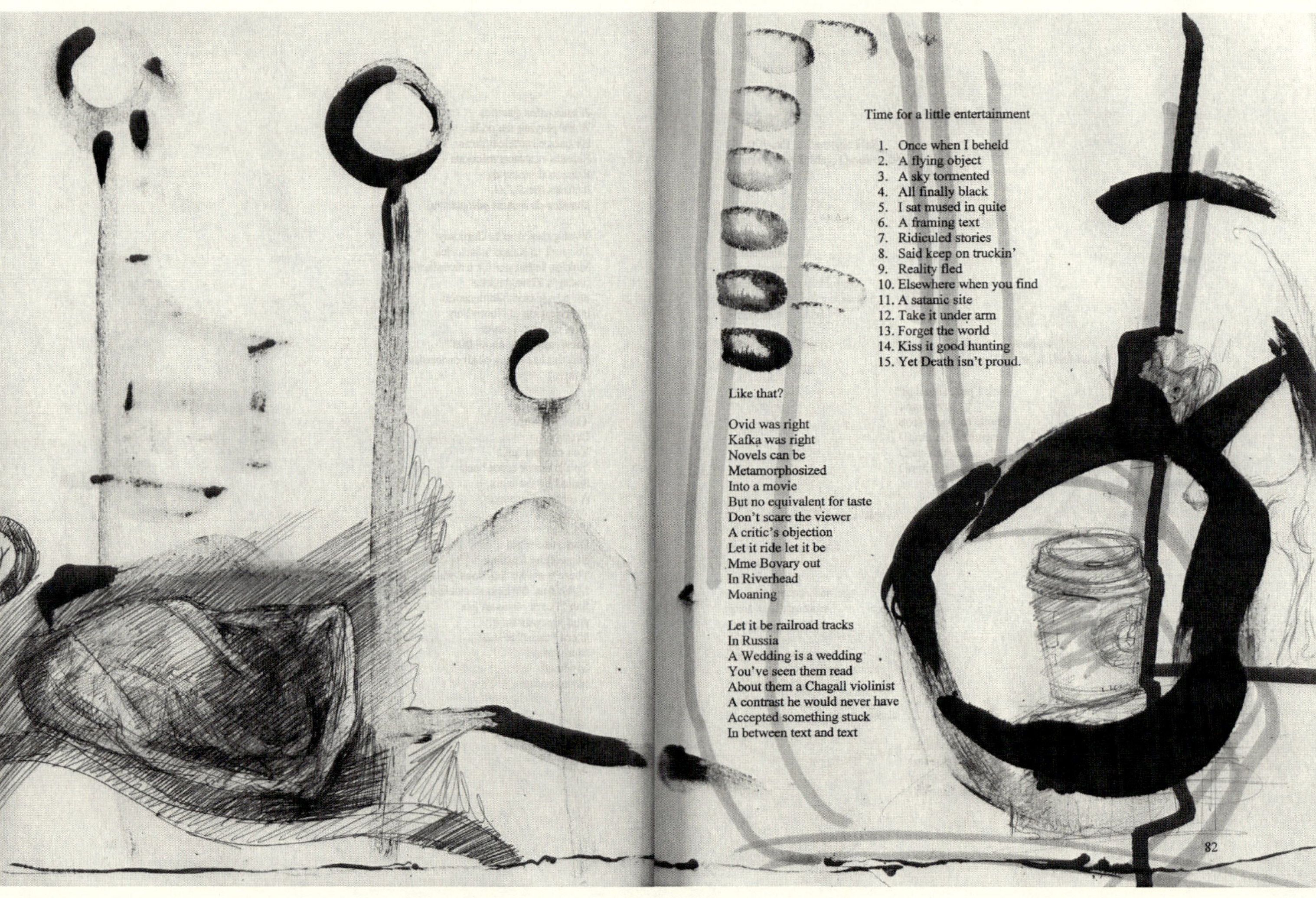

Time for a little entertainment

1. Once when I beheld
2. A flying object
3. A sky tormented
4. All finally black
5. I sat mused in quite
6. A framing text
7. Ridiculed stories
8. Said keep on truckin'
9. Reality fled
10. Elsewhere when you find
11. A satanic site
12. Take it under arm
13. Forget the world
14. Kiss it good hunting
15. Yet Death isn't proud.

Like that?

Ovid was right
Kafka was right
Novels can be
Metamorphosized
Into a movie
But no equivalent for taste
Don't scare the viewer
A critic's objection
Let it ride let it be
Mme Bovary out
In Riverhead
Moaning

Let it be railroad tracks
In Russia
A Wedding is a wedding
You've seen them read
About them a Chagall violinist
A contrast he would never have
Accepted something stuck
In between text and text

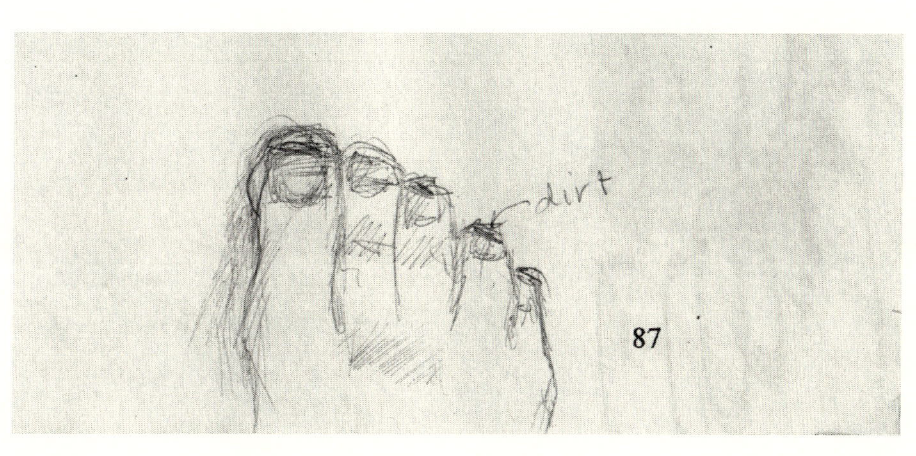

87

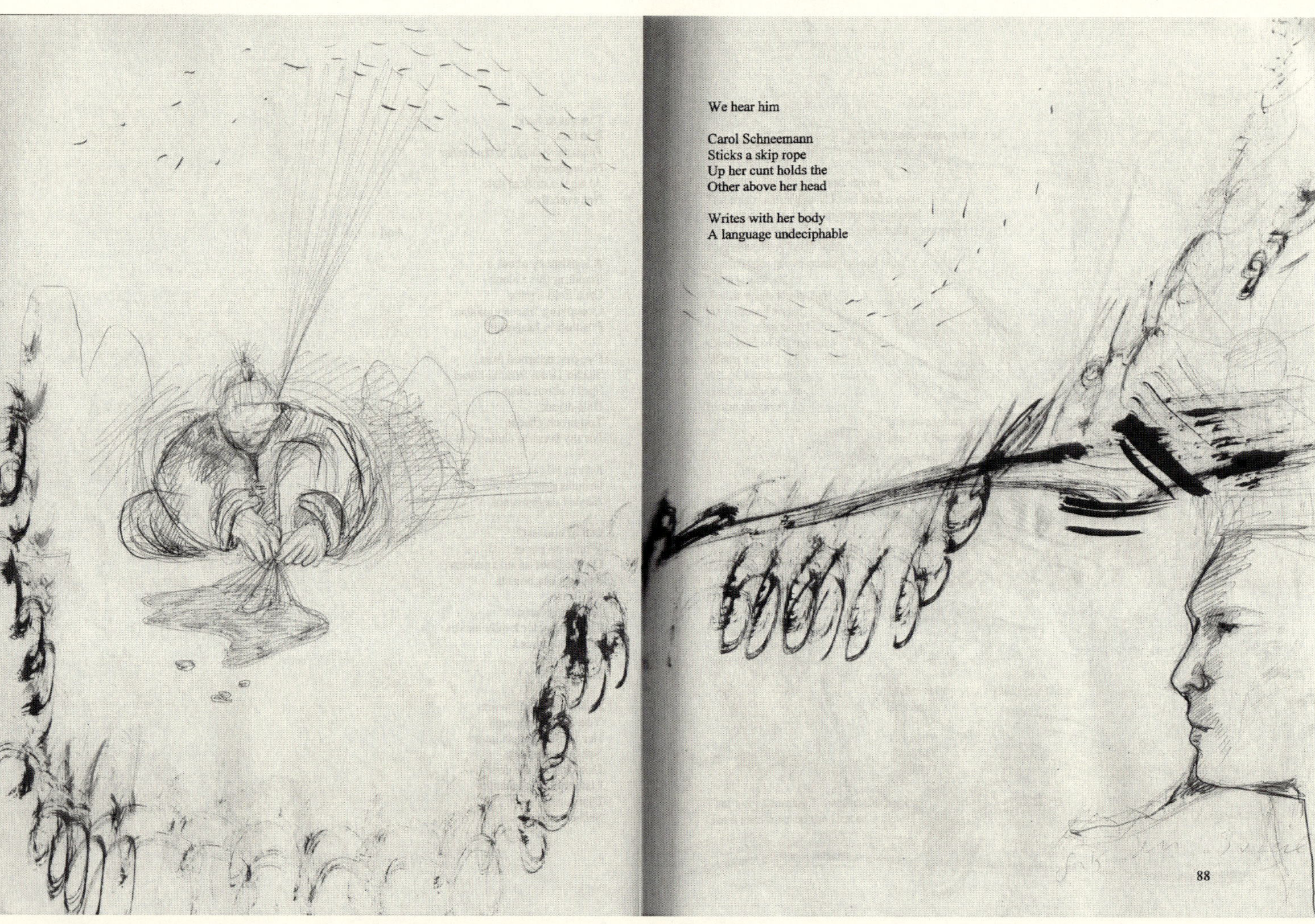

We hear him

Carol Schneemann
Sticks a skip rope
Up her cunt holds the
Other above her head

Writes with her body
A language undecipihable

XXI.

Long
Tailed
Huge
PHALLUS

Bordeaux wines

Forest dancing

Moon

Her stepson
Hatred

Tuthmosis III

O Mother
Into
History

Sun's shining
Man strikes

Enemies all
Around
Blissful
Perfumed
Ready to go
To
War

Seated
Woman
Means AIR WIND or SAIL

And

Leaning
A window open

John Ruskin "Of Tunerian Light"

Lowdown and out

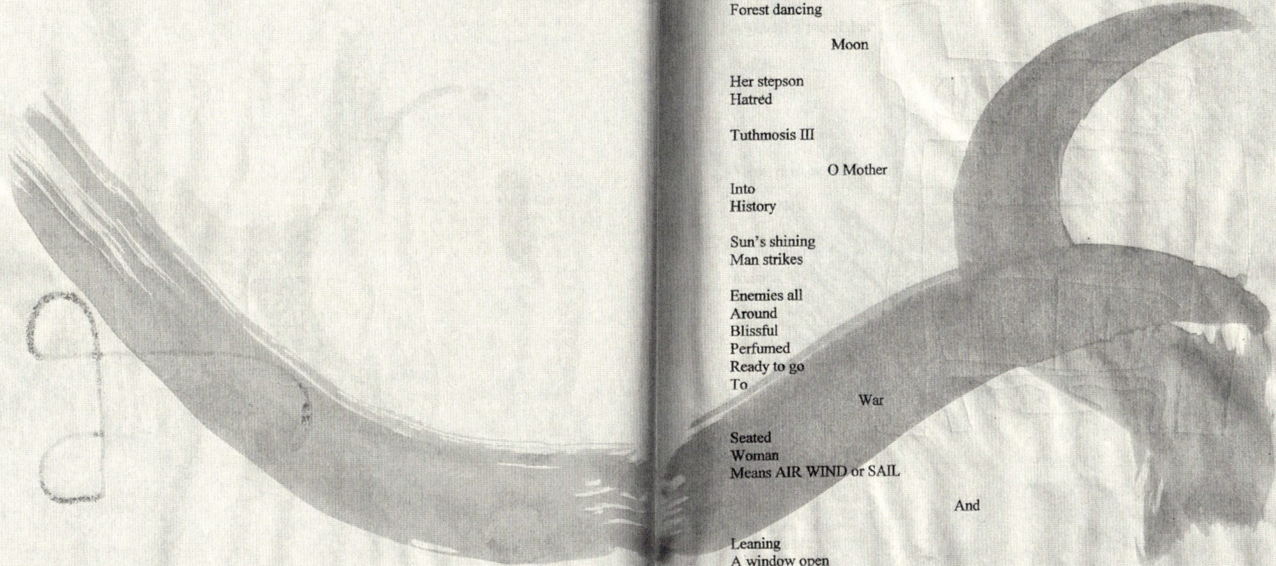

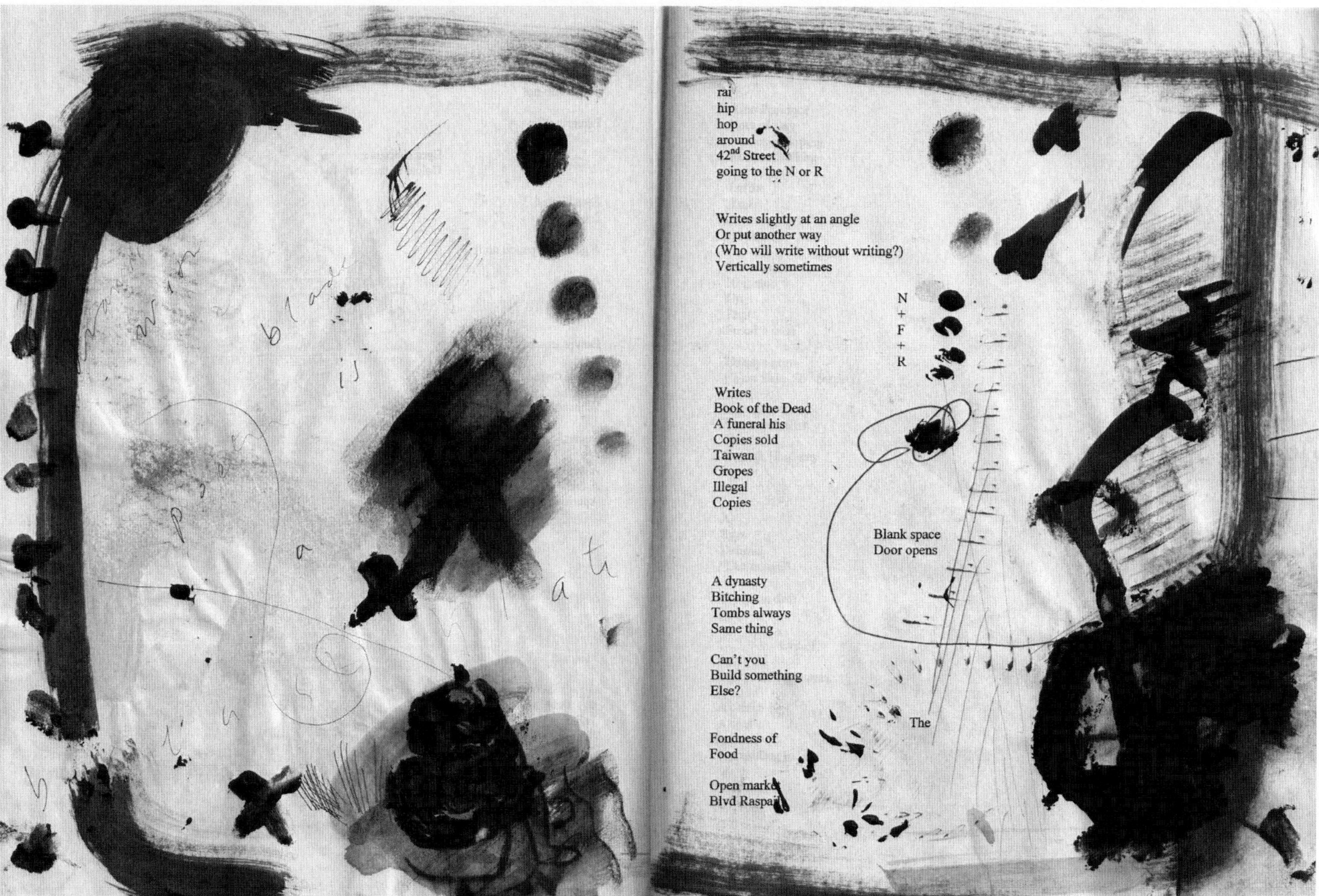

rai
hip
hop
around
42nd Street
going to the N or R

Writes slightly at an angle
Or put another way
(Who will write without writing?)
Vertically sometimes

N
+
F
+
R

Writes
Book of the Dead
A funeral his
Copies sold
Taiwan
Gropes
Illegal
Copies

Blank space
Door opens

A dynasty
Bitching
Tombs always
Same thing

Can't you
Build something
Else?

The

Fondness of
Food

Open market
Blvd Raspail

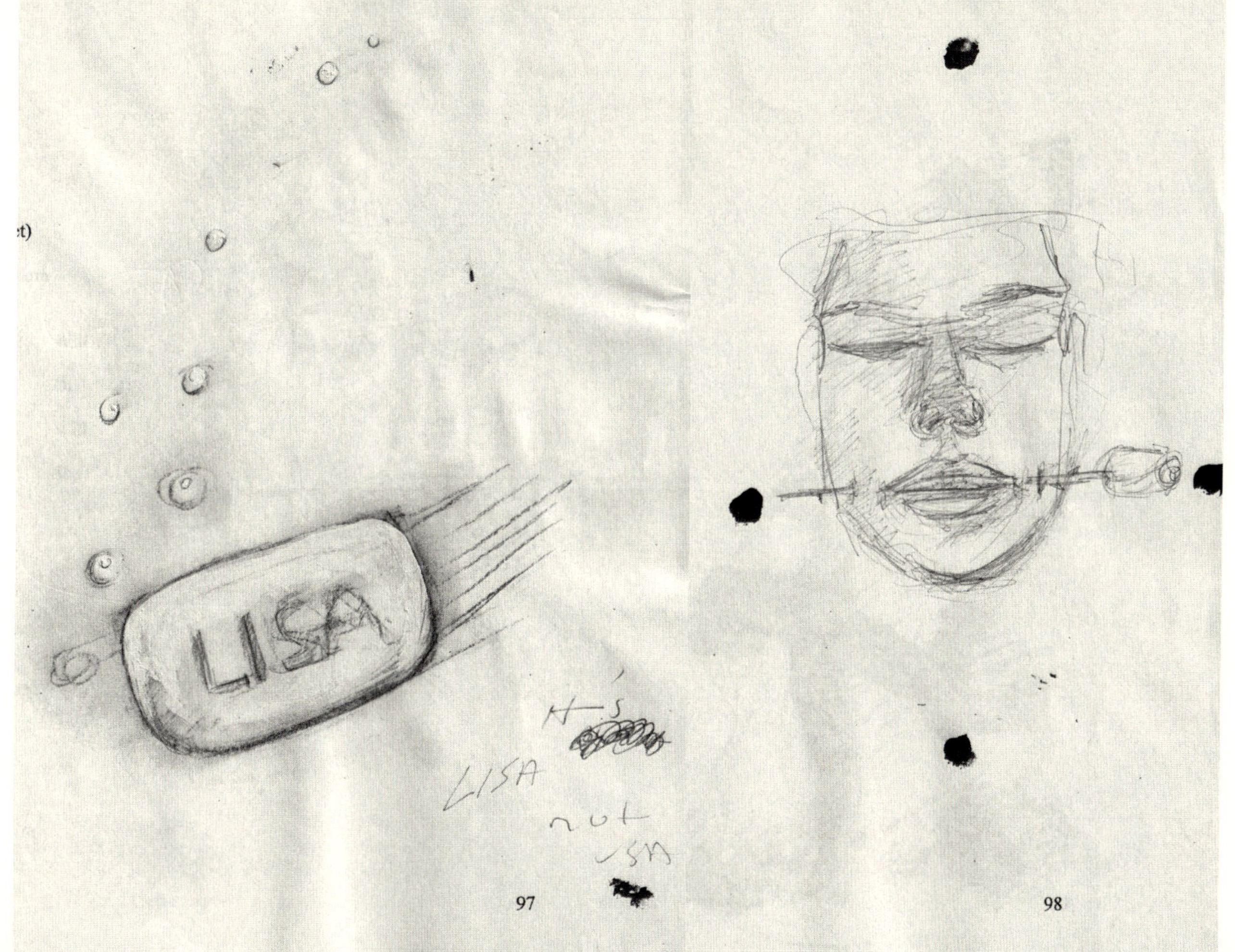

97

98

(then creeping "back" early
times infancy?)

All seemed faced
By a decision
A flatness a voice
No emotions this time round

INTERMISSION:

A 15 line poem

1. Joe's life is a *liebestod*
2. He walks down Sunset Blvd
3. Otherwise nothing to watch
4. His flat TV screen screaming
5. A double life in private
6. "The moon is like the moon"
7. Despite rotten translations
8. A blur a misplaced metaphor
9. She heard existence refused
10. A memory disputed
11. Asked again whose fault is it
12. I told you she answered
13. Did you know knowledge hurts
14. Call quickly for bonus miles
15. Check the island of desire.

End of poem

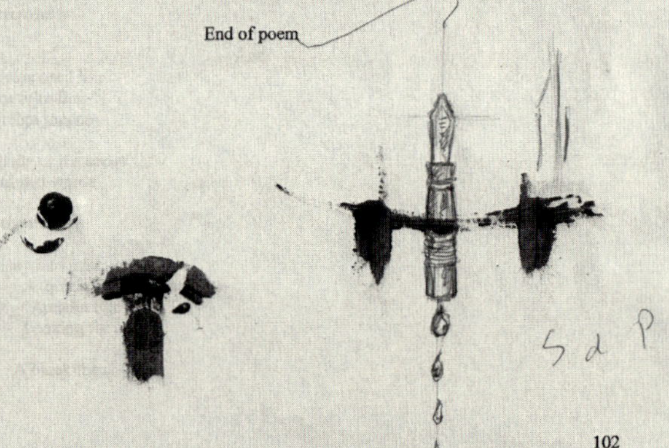

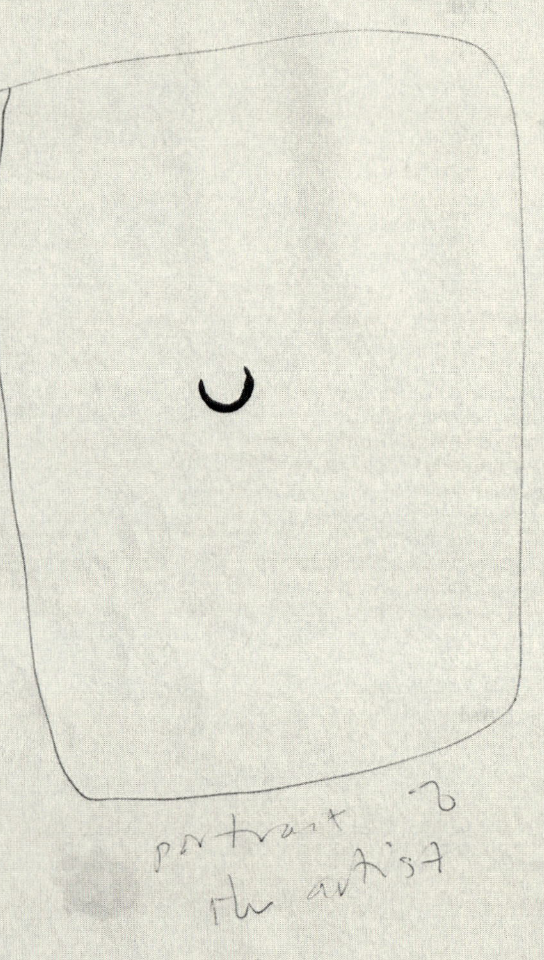

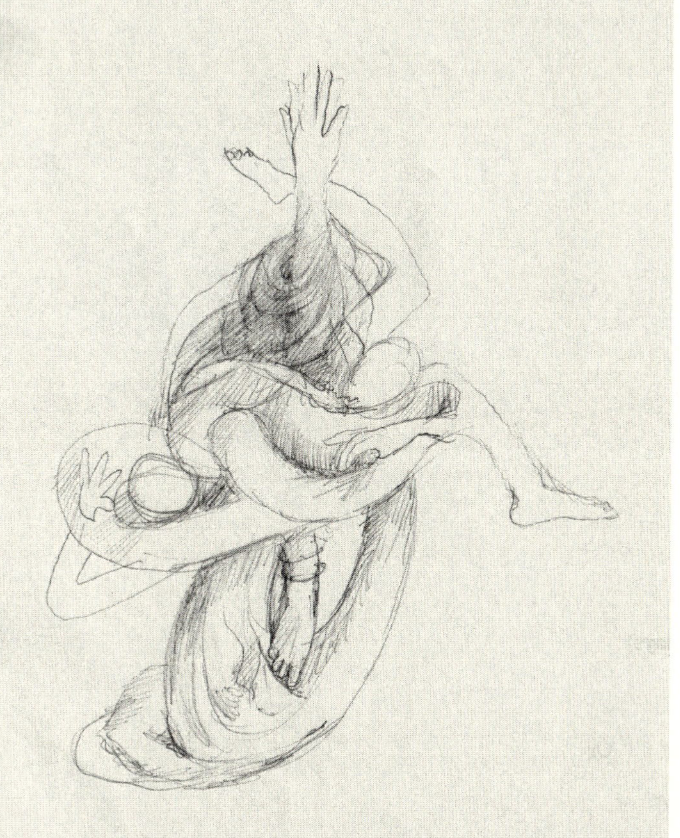

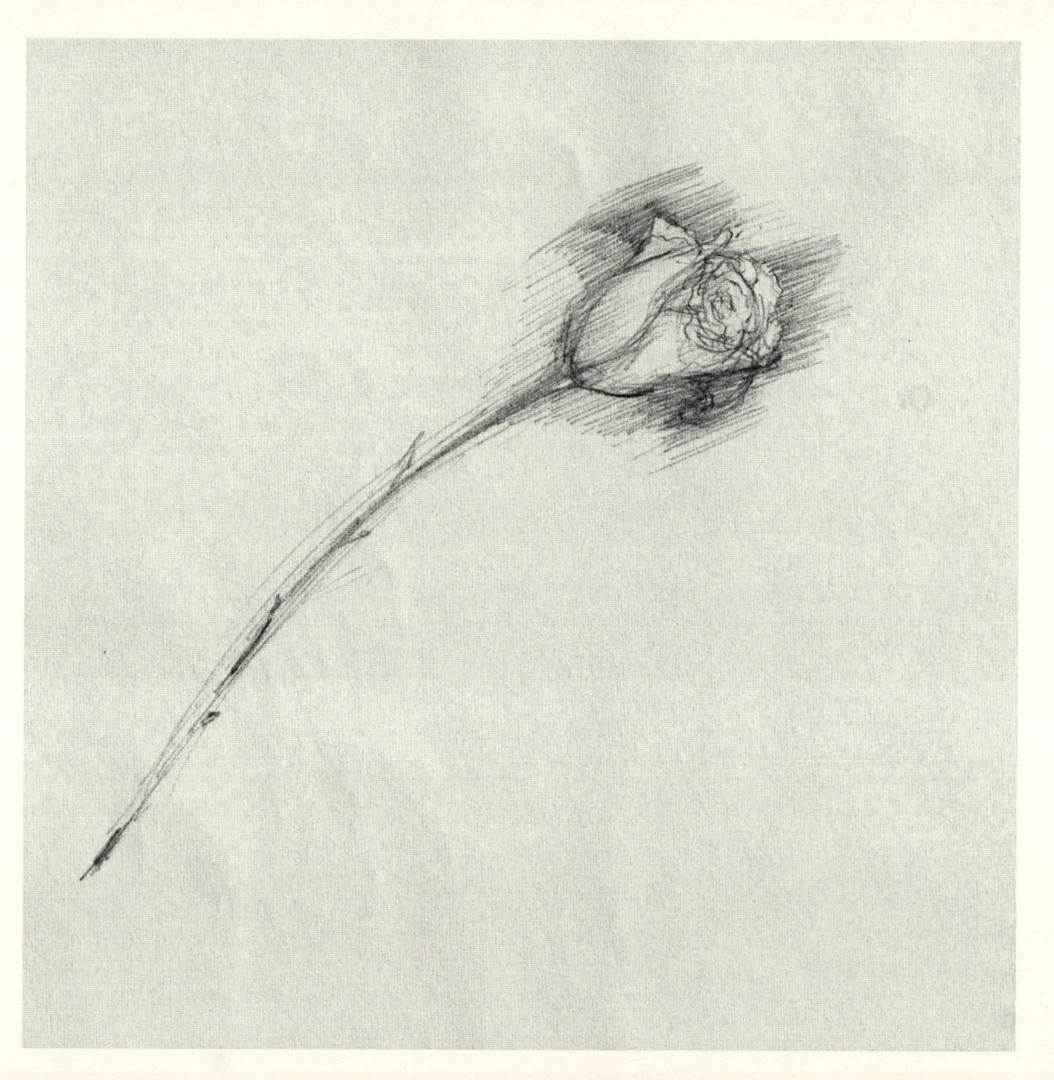

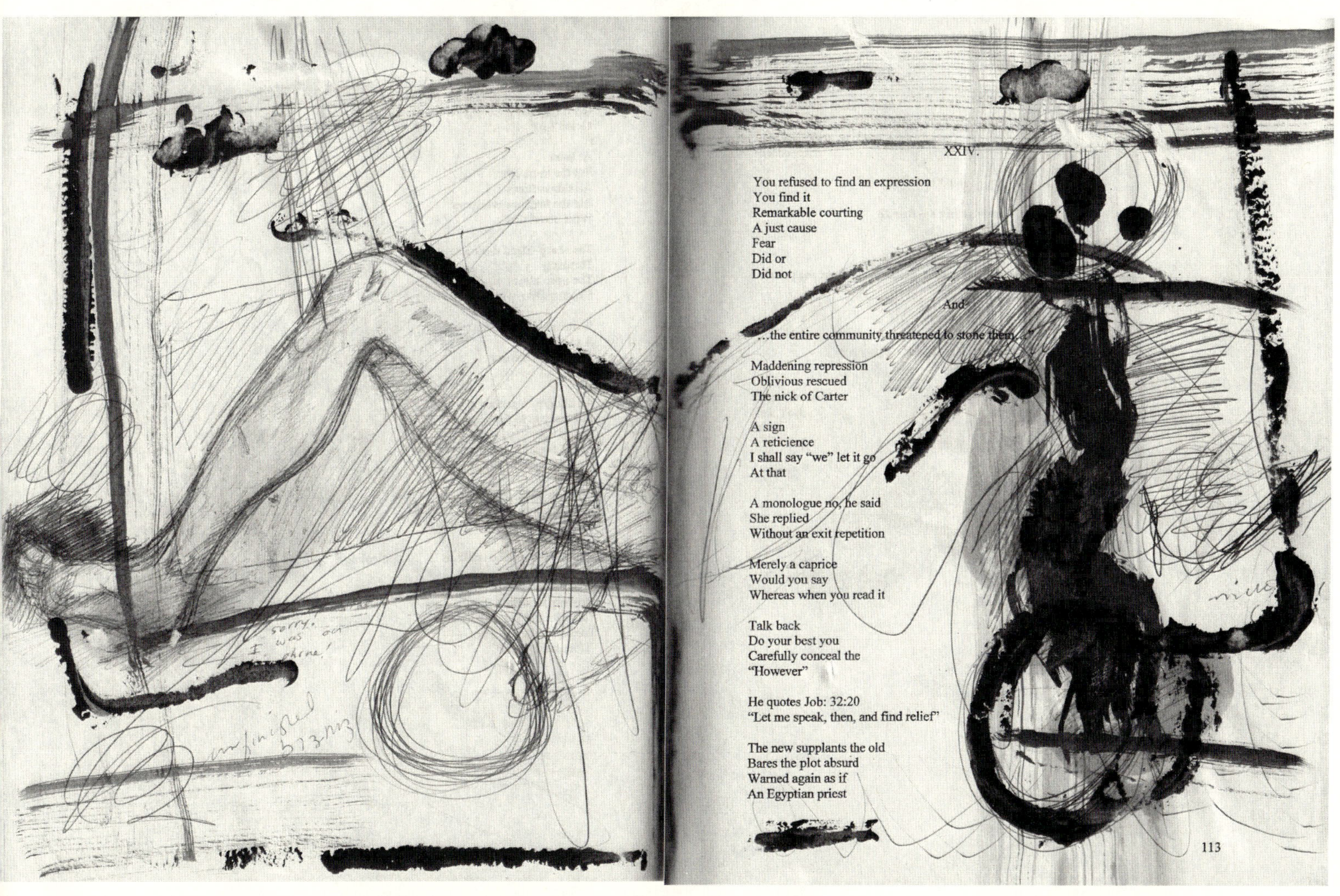

XXIV.

You refused to find an expression
You find it
Remarkable courting
A just cause
Fear
Did or
Did not

And

…the entire community threatened to stone them…"

Maddening repression
Oblivious rescued
The nick of Carter

A sign
A reticience
I shall say "we" let it go
At that

A monologue no, he said
She replied
Without an exit repetition

Merely a caprice
Would you say
Whereas when you read it

Talk back
Do your best you
Carefully conceal the
"However"

He quotes Job: 32:20
"Let me speak, then, and find relief"

The new supplants the old
Bares the plot absurd
Warned again as if
An Egyptian priest

THE AUTHOR

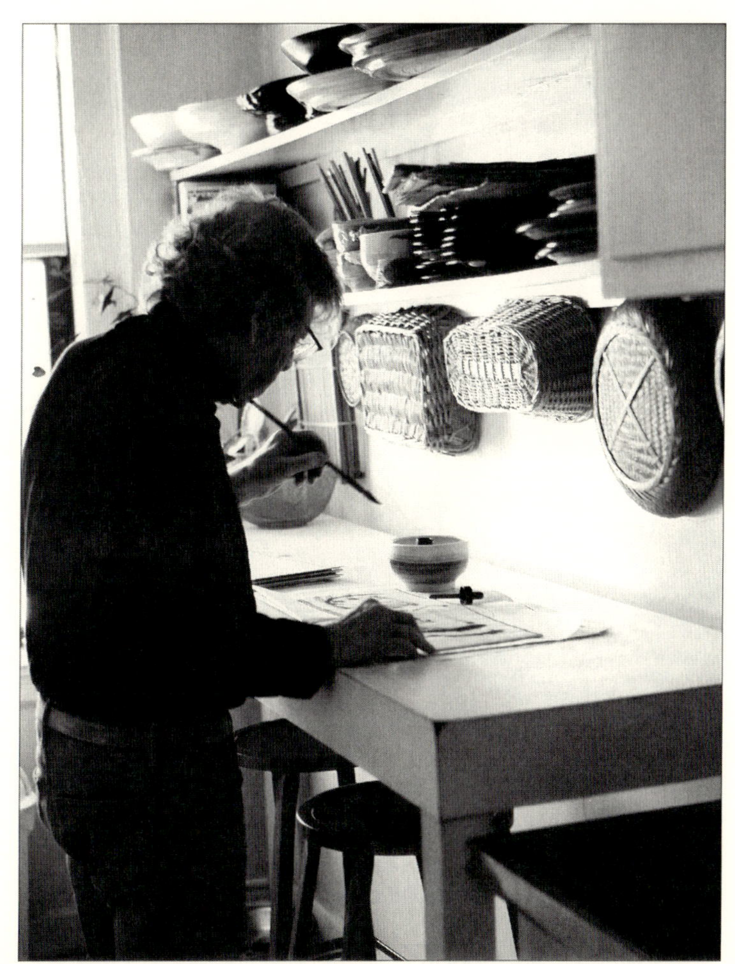

THE PRESS

Chax Press has always sought to bring a sense of expanded possibility to the book, acted out in design, typography. sometimes materials and structures. We began in 1984 and have published some 250 books, including artists' books, fine press books, hybrid letterpress-digital books, chapbooks, trade paperback books, and casebound or boxed publications. In 2021 the Chax Press director received the Lord Nose Award (named in honor of the legendary Jonathan Williams of The Jargon Society), conferred by the Community of Literary Magazines and Presses, for lifetime achievement in literary publishing.

Please join our mission by supporting Chax. You will find us online at *https://chax.org*, and you can email us at *chaxpress@chax.org*. Correspondence to the press should be sent to
Chax Press / 1517 N Wilmot Rd no. 264 / Tucson AZ 85712 / USA.